HALLOWEEN

Oklahoma Tricks and Treats

1900 - 1989

Marilyn A. Hudson

DEDICATION

Many thanks go to the people who shared their memories of Halloween for this project. The family stories, anecdotes, and other 'doings' have been very valuable in capturing the 'spirit' of the holiday.

And, as agreed, I have kept your names private to avoid your families learning what rascals you really were!

I have included a listing of news articles from the Oklahoma City area for the time. This subject bibliography will allow anyone to read further about this topic or do more in-depth research related to several related topics.

As a subject at the edges of society, marginalized as a children's activity, or denigrated due to a belief system, Halloween with its emphasis on the imaginary, has much to say about real life in Oklahoma.

CONTENTS

INTRODUCTION

I recall as a child the eager anticipation as the trees turned to gold, scarlet, and brown beneath an October sky with a unique clarity and a deep azure color. The time of fall festivals, bags of candy, parties, hayrides, mad leaps into piles of crackling eaves, and lots of plain fun.

The inspiration for dozens of daring deeds and funny pranks from older adults and siblings and delightful shivers danced up spines as scary stories and stupid jokes were shared around glowing jack-a-lanterns.

There was the giggling excitement of heading to the local Woolworths or Ben Franklin to see the long rows of shiny boxes, each with a small window of hard cellophane revealing wondrous masks for fairies, heroes, and animals. The hard decisions that followed: would it be the exotic gypsy fortuneteller or the Little Red Riding Hood, or maybe the Monster, Clown, or a Spaceman this year? Every child readily over looked the shortcomings of the mandatory accompanying acetate satin costume (always for some reason with sparkles detailing the seams and adding details to the costume). To short or too long, what did matter?

It was Halloween!

Halloween and numerous rites of passage lay ahead with each new turning of the season.

Arcane knowledge and childhood rituals passed from generation to generation: look for the sacred light of welcome (the front porch light casting its feeble glow), look carefully before you cross the street, and always, always say "Thank you."

HALLOWEEN

Anticipatory huddles preceded the event on playgrounds, street corners, and in back yards. Skills were shared in excited whispers, but ultimately it was a lonely hero's journey to be faced in solitude. A rite of passage was learning to walk boldly up the forbidden zone of someone's front porch, climbing nervously the steps illuminated by glowing jack-o-lanterns knocking on a door that stood ten feet tall.

A soft childish knock, a stuttering "trick-or-treat!" followed by smiling faces, mock looks of surprise or fear at your dime store or homemade costume. The handfuls of goodies dumped into plastic pumpkins, paper bags, or mother's second best pillowcases. Squeaky voices excitedly calling "thank you!" Children rushing back to the sidewalk to catch up with friends. Voices mingling in squeals of delight, as they compared their booty, and autumn joined in blowing chill kisses and swirling her colorful skirt.

Halloween is a distinctly American holiday. Its taproots stem from ancient rituals and celebrations. The manner in which it developed was unique and reflected the "melting pot" s many cultures met and mingled.

As the celebration changed, one element remained at the core: the festival belongs to the land of the imagination: that rich, fertile soil, from which all creativity stems and innovation flows.

Although every decade saw some threat to produce enjoy the season but sanity prevailed and the joys of this special rite continued, changed perhaps by contemporary influences, truncated through modern fears, but it remains as a reminder that people – of al ages – need magic, mystery, and hours of simple fun.

1 ORIGINS

I love October...the crunchy leaves, the chilly nights...and the drama and imagination of Halloween. I was one of those little kids that lived in dress-up clothes, tripped around her mother's heels and should have won an Oscar at some point in Kindergarten for my stellar performance of Little Red Riding Hood.

I am also an American Celt...no I have no real language or the major customs, but there were a bunch of Celts in my family tree. Despite the lack of language and a loss of many customs...the blood runs strong in other ways. The poet is alive, the warrior, the dreamer, and...Face it...maybe even a tad bit of the schemer. There is also the mystic who can step out into a night and *almost* see the shimmering layers that curtain us from other realities, as they ripple in some cosmic breeze.

Halloween began as such in a long distant time. It was a night when someone would leave the door between this world and the next ajar. The recently dead, and perhaps other things, could come to call. Saucers of milk would be left out as an offering to keep the visit...friendly.

So enjoy the sigh of the wind and the crackle of leaves as you walk. Set out your autumn decorations and enjoy the "October country" as author Ray Bradbury called it...but leave some milk out on the night. Just in case.

Now some history; to understand the roots of Halloween it is necessary introduce the Celts.

The term Celts refer to numerous tribal groups occupying Europe from about 800 C.E. who shared a common language group. From the Steppes to Ireland they were the tradesman, philosophers, artisans, and warriors who dominated the landscape and successfully challenged early Rome. They were the ancestors of the people known as the "Gauls", the "Norseman", and the "Britons". Although they shared a common language and fundamental religious beliefs, they developed in many different ways and practices varied.

One common belief held by many of these people groups was that on a particular night of the year the separation of this world from the next changed.

Like a curtain billowing in a breeze glimpses between the two co-existing realities were possible. Sometimes, the recently dead could slip back into the world of the living to say goodbyes, give a blessing, or cause a bit of mischief.

For the Celts, most of whom believed in reincarnation, death was but another part of existing. Customs of leaving small gifts to not offend the returning dead (and bring about problems) often developed. Animals were favored forms for the returning dead and so leavings milk out for dogs or cats became the custom in some locations.

All of this occurred at the turning of the year at Samhaim (Sow-wain). Harvest time the world over share similar festivals marking the end of the growing season, the successful gathering of the harvest, and celebration before the onslaught of winter's stark chill.

Yet, the idea of ghosts goes back much further.

In one of the world's oldest writings, *The Odyssey*, attributed to Homer in the 8th century BCE, there is an interesting scene of Hades with dark blood and pale specters. Interestingly, the ghosts are described as, *".. spirit, like a dream, flits away, and hovers to and fro"* and elsewhere as *"pale and wavering"*......

In the midst of his struggle to return home, the hero sacrifices rams and summons one particular shade, but others come as well.

They are drawn by the sacrificial blood and the life it represents...spectral moths to a flame of mortality. It is very interesting that this - so old a tale - contains some of the same motifs so common to modern beliefs of ghosts. The ability of the death's shade to move in non-human ways, to appear opaque, and to be drawn to those who can see them. Numerous alleged mediums indicate that this is a danger whenever people play with games or relics designed to contact the dead....the door is opened and there are no guarantees as to what may tag along.....

Surely, the vampire legends also see their roots in this older image as well...the glistening, dark, rich blood that brings the dead like famished, thirsting wanderers of the dark desert of death.

Stories have always helped humans to describe, define, and decode the mysteries of their existence. People have always loved to gather to hear and share tales of romance, daring, and mystery. So it should not be too unusual that some themes and symbols become common motifs (what folklorists call archetypes) shared by culturally and geographically diverse peoples.

So, as the next season of ghosts and goblins appears, give a nod of the pumpkin juice to one interesting, and very literary forebearer, and have a Homeric Halloween.

Many of these Celtic customs came to America in early Colonial days, mingling with customs from the Dutch, the English, the Germans, and the Native Americans. There was even an element of the Roman feast of Saturnalia in how America celebrated the night; roles were reversed and chaos celebrated. Many aspects of this initially agrarian based festival would remain important and be kept alive in remote rural areas well into the 20th century. The greatest diversity occurs as locales become increasingly urbanized and more multicultural in the early years of the 20th century.

In Oklahoma, which did not become a state until 1907, there is distinct evidence of the old customs and the melting pot in action as customs from various times, and places begin to mingle and what emerges is the American Halloween. Evidence of this is revealed by the various names over the years: fall festival, harvest festival, "huskin' time", "begging night", "Nutcrack Night" (a term from Britain), Halloween, and even for the more negative, "Helloween."

2 EARLY DAYS AND SIMPLE WAYS (1890-1909)

On Hallowe'en the thing / you must do / Is pretend that nothing can frighten you/ An' if somethin' scares you / and you want to run/ Jus' let on like it's Hallowe'en fun. - Early Nineteenth Century Halloween Postcard

Before and after statehood (1907), the autumn brought many rural pleasures into the spotlight. Long after many moved into the "cities", these agricultural based customs would prevail as a standard for "good, clean fun".

Corn Snapping's or Husking Bees: Crops of corn were placed in piles on a barn or shed floor. Teams of young people would race to strip the dry outer leaves (husks) and their "silk", the thin strands of sticky plant material, from the ears of corn. Special prizes were often awarded for those lucky people who pulled from the piles of ears of all red or all black kernels.

Apple Paring Time: From the fruit of the orchards would come bushels of apples and as winter neared it was important to can, dry, press, or cook these for the long cold days ahead. Rows of canning jars, vats for making apple butter, apple sauce, or spiced apple rings might be part of an evening's party.

Young girls, and sometimes boys, would try their hand at peeling the apple skins from the tasty meat. Young girls were instructed in the mythology of divining future husbands based on how many times you could twist the stem of the apple while reciting the alphabet. This was, according to tales told, a time when a girl might speed up the recitation or slow it down in order to achieve her desired goal! Another way of telling the future was the girl who could peel the apple in one long strip without it breaking was sure to be married the next year.

One has to wonder if this was a stamp of approval on womanly arts; a rite that announced a girl was ready for the work of a wife. In that case, it may have served as a self-fulfilling prophecy.

Baked Surprises: Another custom found was baking into a cake a surprise token (a coin or something similar). The lucky one who received the piece with the surprise, all agreed, was sure to marry in the next year.

Stirring Ashes: This custom was remembered by some but without clear details, but may be similar to reading tea leaves. The ashes in the fire were stirred and futures foretold.

Decorations in this time were homemade, simple, and inexpensive. Popular were Japanese lanterns, fall leaves (real if nature obliged and cut outs if not), jack-o-lanterns, stalks of corn, cut outs of black cats, witch hats, and ghosts.

In some regions, such 'frivolities' or 'play parties' were frowned upon by serious minded folk. Also, some religious groups frowned on such parties, the hint of paganism and witchcraft, or the accompanying activities of dancing, talking, and walking openly between the sexes.

3 Ah, The Good Old Days!

(1910-1919)

From ghoulish and ghosties and long leggety beasties and things that go bump in the night, Good Lord, deliver us! - - - Scottish saying

Once the harvest was in, and the long days of summer were retreating, minds and hands turned to preparing the farm and the small towns for the coming winter. In the crisp air that promised autumn would soon be arriving, many a young mind was on a variety of traditional pastimes: Corn husking parties, harvest festivals, taffy pulls, simple pleasures, fortune telling tephromancy (by ashes) or by the divinations of apple cores, unwinding yard, or a coin in a piece of cake.

Parents worried about-frightened cows and chickens, overturned outhouses, and missing garden gates. Gates appeared to be of special appeal to small boys as they were easy to lift and carry off. Older boys and girls were known to pile gates, scrap wood into the center of intersections and set them ablaze. Annually, local constables fretted over all the promised 'shenanigans' of the local 'hooligans'.

In 1907, one writer for the local Oklahoma City newspaper reflected that things had changed since they were a child. It would be a refrain heard each and every decade as one generation ruminated about the great fun they had, the better quality of the fun in their own day, or the general state of wild abandon found in modern desolate youth. Remember though that somebody had to be instilling these traditions into the minds of the young people coming up from decade to decade; older siblings, grandparents and others helping continue the traditions.

So closely tied to familiar harvest activities and frivolities, the activities were largely rural in nature. They carried with them an aura of acceptable custom that most supported in theory if not always in fact. Despite all the complaints all the actions of youth were still largely innocent, if a bit devilish, fun.

That began to change as the real specters of war and disease struck the home front in the 1916-1919 period.

Influenza, or the 'flu', cut a swathe through the armies of all sides of the European conflict. Communities back home saw sometimes-dire local warnings or threats of canceling activities, even church services, due to fear of contagion.

Believed to have begun in an army camp in Kansas, *"The influenza pandemic of 1918-1919 killed more people than the Great War, known today as World War I (WWI), at somewhere between 20 and 40 million people. It has been cited as the most devastating epidemic in recorded world history. More people died of influenza in a single year than in four-years of the Black Death Bubonic Plague from 1347 to 1351"* (http://virus.stanford.edu/uda/). More are thought to have died from illness than bullets; "1918 influenza pandemic caused at least 675,000 U.S. deaths and up to 50 million deaths worldwide."

Marilyn A. Hudson

(http://www.pandemicflu.gov/general/whatis.html).

One of the common myths associated with Halloween may have its roots in stories torn from newspapers. German and Allied forces both claimed the daring bi-plane pilots tossed 'poisoned candy' down on unsuspecting people during the war. What may have been a story with some truth was more probably manipulated for the propaganda opportunities it provided than for any real death by candy scenarios.

Sources:

"Fate-Finding fun for Halloween." The Oklahoman. (Oct. 29, 1905): 18.

"Halloween at Chickasha" Nov. 1, 1906): 2.

"Citizens Ask Police To Suppress Young Hoodlums." The Oklahoman (Nov. 28, 1906): 7.

"Children Arrested; Stay Out Too Late." The Oklahoman (July 5, 1907): 5.

"Arrest Hallowe'en Raiders After Boiling Water Fight." The Oklahoman (Nov.1, 1907): 8.

"Mutiny is Threatened by "Co-Eds": Girls who paraded in white, penalized and revolt." The Oklahoman (Nov. 2, 1907): 1.

"Seeress' Vision a Trifle Too Late." The Oklahoman. (Oct. 31, 1907) 6.

"Witches will be Abroad in the Land; Next Thursday will be Hallowe'en and Goblins Are Due." The Oklahoman (Oct. 27, 1907): 13.

"New State Notes" The Oklahoman (Nov. 16, 1907): 20.

"Goblins On Parade Tonight." The Oklahoman (Oct. 31, 1908): 5.

"Superstitions". The Oklahoman. (Dec. 12, 1909);41.

"Evil Spirits to Stalk in Night: Yearly Carnival of Gate Stealing and Bad Jokes *coming.." The Oklahoman (Oct. 28, 1909): 5.*

4 "Helloween" vs "Halloween" (1920-1929)

Tis now the very witching time of night, When churchyards yawn and hell itself breathes out Contagion to this world. - - -William Shakespeare

The simple rural pleasures of continuing old world customs of lifting gates and soaping windows began to change according to local newspapers. "Vandalism" began to be used to describe the annual activities of youth in the towns and cities of the state and the nation. More people are moving into towns and cities from collapsed or folded farms, while Immigrant numbers are increasing as well. A generation of "city-folk" emerges in places, like Oklahoma City, who have never lived on a farm.

The normal rhythms of rural life, rural skill building, and rural responsibilities that led to maturity are being replaced by urban events and attitudes. Now schools, and civic policies, seem prone to keep those under a certain age childlike for a long time. The "teen" years are beginning to develop – that long lonely landscape of being neither child nor adult that leads inevitably to boredom and rambunctious actions.

The social caste system was very evident in the 1920's: class, gender, race, politics, and economics divided society. Papers carried announcements detailing plans for Halloween parties for community socialites, parties to which most of society would never be able to attend, further segmented the population. Large urban hotels specialized in elegant parties with costume prizes and music bands offering up familiar foxtrots and the latest in 'hot jazz'. Others, the up and coming and the already arrived business classes, held more intimate get-togethers that were just as well attended, enjoyed, and flaunted.

These class struggles reflect a time when Socialism takes its first major grip in the United States, challenging even the major political parties with new solutions to an old set of problems. The excesses of the roaring years and the collapse of an economy were heralded as signs of the inevitable conquest of capitalism by communist socialism.

The often boastful details of parties and events on the society pages of newspapers was a reinforcement of the caste system and a reflection of the decade that would be marked by its spiraling out of control excesses. Yet, one of the reasons newspapers filled their pages with such news was because it sold papers. The lower classes and those above sought news and inspiration for their own life. No doubt, many a booming success of later years found their dreams born in reading about the community gentry and saying, "that will be me someday."

Sources:

"Fix the Pumpkin Hallowe'en Near: "Nutcrack Night" to be Observed in the Metropolis Monday, Oct. 31." The Oklahoman (Oct. 24, 1910): 5.

"Hop Joint Raid; Twelve Arrested." The Oklahoman (Dec. 14, 1910): 16.

"Editorial: The Carnival Spirit of Hallowe'en." The Oklahoman (Oct. 30, 1910); 32.

"Nutcrack Night Keeps Cops Busy." The Oklahoman (Nov. 1, 1910) :10.

"Ad: Masks for Halloween." The Oklahoman. (Oct. 22, 1915): 7.

"Sheets and Shouts Replace Usual Halloween Vandalism; Arrests Few, Warnings Many." The Oklahoman. (Nov. 1, 1916): 1.

"Old Glory Carnival at Yukon October 31". The Oklahoman (Oct. 30, 1917): 13.

"Kansas Man Shot Boy on Halloween." The Oklahoman. (Nov. 2, 1917): 12.

"NO "Ghosts" To Be Out Halloween: "Flu" Epidemic Interferes with Customary Pranks." The Oklahoman. (Oct. 20, 1918): 14.

"Ad", ibid, pg. 9.

"The 1918 Influenza Pandemic of 1918." http://virus.stanford.edu/uda/ (accessed 6/1/08).

"What is an Influenza ...?" at Pandemic Flu http://www.pandemicflu.gov/general/whatis.html

1920-1929

"Ad: Hallowe'en". The Oklahoman (Oct. 28, 1921): 14.

"Hallowen Eve Costume Dance. (AD)"The Oklahoman (Oct. 28, 1921):

14.

"Chickens Make Home in Old Foss Jail: Violators of Law Must Go to Cordell". The Oklahoman (Nov. 29, 1921): 4.

"Hallowe'en." The Oklahoman (Oct. 29, 1922): 59.

"Hallowe'en Origin Back in Dim Past". The Oklahoman (Oct. 22, 1922): 10.

"Big, Red Apples for Halloween" (AD). The Oklahoman (Oct. 30, 1923): 5.

"Youth to Make Merry Tonight, on Hallowe'en." The Oklahoman (Oct. 31, 1922): 12.

"Pranksters Are Few, Say Cops." The Oklahoman (Oct. 29, 1923): 3.

"Okmulgee Has Wild Hallowe'en Frolic." The Oklahoman (Nov. 2,1925): 3.

"Hallowe'en Booth" (AD) The Oklahoman (Oct. 29, 1926):22.

"Hallowe'en Jokes Do Little Damage." The Oklahoman (Nov. 1, 1926): 20

"Halloween Fete is Planned at Enid." The Oklahoman (Oct. 9, 1929): 17.

"Halloween Is Observed With Party: Dr. and Mrs. John Payne Entertain for Their Daughter." The Oklahoman. (Oct. 28, 1929): 6.

5 Safe and Sensible Days (1930-1939)

Where there is no imagination there is no horror.

- - -Sir Arthur Conan Doyle

With the depression, the 1930's were a challenge to vast segments of the population to just survive, let alone celebrate a holiday. Yet, that is often when it is seen that keeping customs alive bring hope for the good times to return.

In 1930, Halloween was a gooey mess when a well blew and spouted oil all over Northeast Oklahoma City. It seemed portentous for some, with the recent economic downturn of 1929, known vividly as 'the crash', that the incident involving the symbol of oil wealth had occurred so near the state capital. The mad wealth of the early oil days, surely could not be in jeopardy? If nothing else, however, it added another layer of excitement to a night already packed with activity.

As always, diligent law officers and concerning community leaders looked to the schools to warn children about being orderly and safe. Added to their warnings would be caution about getting close to open flames in their costumes. The news of children suffering horribly, and even dying, was repeated often to avoid injury.

Rowdy behavior was still the norm and the use of 'children' can be misleading in reading old accounts. For many in this time period, the children were what we might call adolescents or teenagers. Smaller children under the age of ten were usually not part of the groups, according to accounts, that took part in the more interesting events.

For children and youth, feeling the stress and fears of unemployment, poverty, and adult anxiety, the night offered a release. The adults assumed the night was in their control, but most young people knew it really belonged to them. It always had.

Late in the decade, Orson Well's Mercury Theater production of "A War of the Worlds" would add another layer of concern to the holiday. This was a particularly effective broadcast in America due to the war in Europe and the fears of American being brought into another conflict. The invasion scenario, no doubt, caused some people to be a bit conflicted about how they would respond to a real life 'foreign invasion'.

Sources:

"Halloween Costumes". (AD) The Oklahoman (Oct. 26, 1920): 11.

"Woman's Death Attributed to Halloween Explosion." The Oklahoman (Nov. 1, 1930): 1

"True Cauldron of Witches Bubbles Evil Air Over City: Wild Well Spouting on Halloween Night is Appropriate Gesture for the Season." The Oklahoman (Nov.1, 1930): 13.

"It's Time to Take in the Chairs" The Oklahoman. (Oct. 29, 1931): 1.

"Make your Hallowe'en Cake a thriller with Calumet's Double-Action!" (AD) The Oklahoman (Oct. 31, 1931)7.

"Two Children Die as Costumes Burn." The Oklahoman (Nov. 3, 1931)4.

"Halloween Edict Goes to Schools." The Oklahoman (Oct. 28, 1930): 14.

"Death Blamed on Halloween." The Oklahoman (Nov. 2, 1932): 8.

"Sanity Rules Halloween Over All U.S. This Year." The Oklahoman (Oct. 31, 1935. 12.

"School Head Tells of Boy's Death in Halloween Prank." The Oklahoman (Nov. 2, 1935)8.

"Shh! It's Going to Be A Safe and Sane Halloween." The Oklahoman (Oct. 25m 1936)19.

"Ghosts, Soap Witches Too Halloween!" The Oklahoman (Oct. 31, 1936) 10.

"Second Halloween Afflicts Scores of Householders." The Oklahoman (Nov. 1, 1937); 2.

"Police Happy as Halloween Party Plans Are Pushed." The Oklahoman

(Oct. 10, 1937) 79.

"Children's Joy is Helloween to Grownups: Peace Parties Help, but not much. The City is Torn Up." The Oklahoman. (Oct. 31, 1937): 17-18.

"No Nightmare, Just Halloween Spooks." (with photo) The Oklahoman (Oct. 23 1938): 32.

"Men of Mars" Scare Brings Added Threat: Technique Change Promised By Network Heads." The Oklahoman (Nov. 1, 1938)6.

"Clean Halloween Fun to be Police Standard." The Oklahoman (Oct. 30, 1939): 1.

"Little Darlings Give the Folks a Fretful Night: For What they Did on Halloween They Could Go To Jail." Nov. 1, 1939)1.

"Two Letter Writers Stand Up for Modern Halloween Fun." The Oklahoman (Nov. 8, 1939)20.

6 From Delinquents to Deputies (1940-1949)

The rowdy and rambunctious thirties spawned communities who set out to provide engineered and carefully scripted fun for their youth. Almost every community of size set up committees to oversee an evening of varied and tiring activities. Parades, carnivals, fund raising, community projects, costume contests, dances, picnics were among some of the functions placed on the calendars of the 1940's. Some communities were determined that this rampant disregard for community order, known familiarly as Halloween, would be carefully controlled with laws, curfews, and expanded police forces for the duration.

One youth rebelled against the attempt to rob children of their traditional night of party by suing for his right to run amuck through the community. Most, however, merely obeyed, but slipped out after curfews to meet with friends.

Overall, the inward focus on the one holiday did serve to dampen some episodes of high-jinks. It was hard to tell, at times, when newspapers talked about the relative calm of local communities whether they were celebrating or complaining.

All that changed, however, in December of 1941 when reality brought a new seriousness to the minds of almost all. Although fun and laughter were still sought after, there was now a sense of propriety on the matter. When men, some from your own community, were fighting and dying overseas there were more serious matters to be considered.

War effort fundraisers, troop entertainments, and community events were promoted as worthy of support by all the community. Gifts and candy were diverted in some cases to make certain the troops enjoyed a Halloween in the midst of the struggle.

The traditional, and simpler, customs made a come back as all tried to sacrifice for the common good. Although a few youth had their fun despite the dire days and critics called the celebration a "Helloween," most found lots of fun in rediscovering the pleasures of an earlier day.

Sources:

"Work Projects Plan Schools For Streamlining Halloween." The Oklahoman (Oct. 1, 1940)7,

"City is ready for Halloween." The Oklahoman (Oct. 27, 1940):30.

"State Youth Sues for Halloween Fun 'Rights' and $4,000." The Oklahoman (Dec. 6, 1940):5.

"Man From mars Doesn't Drop In." The Oklahoman (Nov. 1, 1940) 6.

"Halloween Quieter or Did you Notice?" The Oklahoman. (Nov. 1, 1940) 1.

"Boys Apologize for Nazi Flag Prank." The Oklahoman (Nov. 17, 1940): 74.

"Parade, Queen Crowning Set for Halloween." The Oklahoman (Oct. 19, 1941): 27.

"Halloween Made easy, Young Imaginations Needn't Strain So." The Oklahoman (Oct. 24, 1941)15.

"Plan an Eerie background for Halloween." The Oklahoman (Oct. 26, 1941):64.

"Fun Without Damage Pleas Made by Smith." The Oklahoman. (Oct. 31, 1942): 3.

"Halloween Parties Are Set by USO". The Oklahoman (Oct. 30, 1943) 5.

"Halloween May Serve War as Well as Youth." The Oklahoman (Oct. 30. 1943)8.

"U.S. Troops Don't Forget Halloween." The Oklahoman (Oct. 31, 1943)44.

"Police Pranks Curbed, Too." The Oklahoman (Oct. 26, 1944)12.

"Police Proud: City Behaves on Halloween." The Oklahoman (Nov. 5, 1944)26.

"Mannerly Halloween Revelers Jam Main With Record Crowd." The Oklahomlan (Nov. 1, 1944)1.

"Tragedy Ends Youth's Joy Ride on Halloween." The Oklahoman (Nov. 5, 1944) 27.

Johnson, Edith. "Why Not a Halloween Instead of Helloween?" The Oklahoman. (Oct. 28, 1944):6.

"Programs Set on Hallowe'en." The Oklahoman. (Oct. 26, 1945) 19.

7 Take Us To Your Leader (1950-1959)

Post world war, the single desire of American society was escape from the turbulence and grief of the battle years. In an eager rush to return things to 'normal', a lot of culture became idealized. This meant a lot of things were redefined by an unnatural reality.

During these years conformity was more important than individualism, the genders split into a hyper-masculinity and a hyper-femininity and strong social forces (similar to the forces at work in the Victorian era) mandated just what was normal, acceptable, or proper. Cookie cutter housing tracks developed as suburbia was born, assembly lines were refitted to provide more of everything, and life generally looked up.

Occasionally, like bubbles in a fermenting swamp, evil peaked out its head in the form of the threat of nuclear annihilation and marauding communism.

A lantern moon smiles down on the balmy night as children in cowboy clothes, pirate hats, hobo rags, or draped sheet cruise the streets of

America. Shouts of recognition and giggles of anticipation fill the cooling night. Neighbors wave to parents with small children standing protectively on the sidewalk. Clusters of costumed figures voice groans of envy comparing bags and sacks of "treats".

No one is a stranger, despite the disguises but everywhere are feigned surprises as identities are revealed. Mr. Smith always comes to the door in a mask and laughs as he dispenses the popcorn balls his wife has made. Each one lovingly wrapped in crisp wax paper and tied with orange and black ribbon by Mrs. Smith herself. Mrs. Johnson always leaves a tub on the porch by a glowing jack-o-lantern with goodies piled high. She and her husband watch with a cup of coffee from the front window and always wave as the children call their appreciation. The Kransky family calls everyone in their large and extended family to the door to see each new trick-or-treater. They guess and laugh as they pile goodies into bags and pour mugs of cider. Dr. Barnes house is spooky looking naturally but on Halloween they add hanging ghosts, corn stalks, and plum pumpkins. Children run from their door in partial delight at the toys added to the candy and a desire to escape alive from the eerie old house.

The old Blaine house in right on the way to the community hall where all the teens are having a dance. It is the solemn duty of every child to show their courage by walking as close to the old house as possible. They demand respect if they walk to the front porch and everyone looks in aw e if they actually made it to the front windows. Most came screaming back telling of horrid and ghostly things seen, real or imagines, through the soapy bedroom windows. Guaranteed hero status is bestowed on any child who actually reaches the front door and peeks in the grimy window at the empty parlors and staircase beyond.

Breathless to escape the creepy old house in one piece they rush to invade the hall where there will be rewards of punch and cookies from the people there. Overall, with heavy bags of sweet loot, UNICEF cartons full of coins, and memories whirling, the night was a success.

Although some sources say 'trick-or-treating" was begun in the post war years, in the 1950's, there was also a general move to replace the night of 'begging' with something more socially redeeming. Various projects, designed to benefit the children of war-torn Europe, were arranged, including the United Nation's collection for the children's fund. Useable clothes, toys, food, and funds were solicited that night by packs of children working together in a manner reminiscent of the war time effort. Some health conscious groups also were skeptical of the nutritious values of such a night of riotous sweets overload.

Costumes were now reflecting the growing popularity of television characters and heroes. A national obsession with cowboys, spacemen, and cartoon figures added a new battalion of possibilities to childish imaginations. Some groups even sought to implement a 'candy' for money program; most children were wisely skeptical. If the adults were willing to give the money to give up candy, more than one reasoned, they better keep the more valuable candy.

The continuing trend to bypass individual or gang shenanigans through community events continued and parades, parties, and events covered the state. In Woodward in 1955 a parade was to feature a seven foot tall robot.

Occasionally an accident occurred, once and a while some kids got carried away, and sometimes people were concerned about the morals of modern youth in just the same way their elders had feared for their own.

The decade also saw a bumper group of children emerge and a new group called teenagers who defied easy identification. As the prosperity of the decade escalated the need for the young person to enter the work force to help support the family decreased just as his social identity as an adult decreased.

These mobile and prosperous youth spawned low-budget and high profit endeavors such as drive-in theaters serving up a menu of movies of rebellion, horror, or science fiction.

Where a previous generation or two easily accepted a sixteen year old as an adult, now they lingered uncomfortably in a twilight zone of not-child and not adult.

Schools operated as stand in parents as the umbrella of social control that locked youth into a prolonged childhood spread ever wider. Sociologists, religious leaders, and psychologists tried to understand why the generation was so geared to be 'A Rebel Without a Cause' or a "Wild One" and never considering they might be the part of the problem.

The "Red Scare", or a Communist in Every Pot, was a major influence in the society of the decade. A real threat had been so magnified it gained a contaminating life of its own. "The Invasion of the Body Snatchers" was a major horror novel adapted for the screen as a vehicle for airing the concerns of those who were hunting the non-conformists in American society. An excellent story gained a patina of too true horror with its social sub-text.

At decade's end an example of the high strangeness of the human condition seemed to confirm fears that not all was well in the world. Ed

Gein was arrested in 1957 and placed in a mental facility. He served as the inspiration for "Psycho" and other films.

Sources

"National Geographic Society: Halloween dates from Barbarism." The Oklahoman (Oct. 23, 1952):19.

"Thieves prowl on Halloween." The Oklahoman (Nov. 1, 1953):29.

"Seven-foot Robot to March in Woodward on Halloween." The Oklahoman (Oct. 30, 1955):72.

"Trick of treat Exchanged for Plea for Funds." The Oklahoman (October 26, 1955):33.

"Friendly Beggar program Planned for Halloween Night." The Oklahoman (Oct. 16, 1956):7.

"Traditional Treats…rejected.." The Oklahoman (Oct. 29, 1957): 12.

True Crime Serial Killers. Alexandria, Va:Time-Life. N.d.

8 TELEVISION TO TERROR
(1960-1969)

'Be wary then: best safety lies in fear.'' Shakespeare, Hamlet.

In the 1960's the concept of the "Spook House" or "Haunted House" began to gain wider popularity. Communities, schools, clubs, and churches were soon sponsoring them. Workers transformed empty buildings, houses, halls, and even stores were soon a popular rage. Despite some early day tragedies in such community haunted houses they persisted as popular attractions.

In the wider society it was a time of revolution as Civil Rights, Vietnam, student protests, increased drug use, and the sexual revolution were creating earthquakes of change. The attempt to totally control childhood continued as the teen years continued to reshape themselves.

Safety was a watchword of the decade as youth were trained in proper street safety, stranger danger, and not getting in with the wrong crowd.

Social pressures, urban overcrowding, poverty and other issues created a sometimes dangerous environment at the best of times in some areas.

Idealistically advisors envisioned a new Halloween based on giving and social responsibility, while news accounts often provided examples of just the opposite. The delinquent to deputy route was re-employed to train younger kids to avoid the risky behaviors of the season.

The idealism was a little tarnished as the end of the decade neared. Unsettling stories reared their heads; stories of apple treats that hid needles, razor blades and similar dire surprises began to circulate and dampen the holiday excitement.

Costumes once more celebrated the hand made touch, often with accessories purchased from the local store. The selection of costumes was now a major process as children mulled their choices of cartoon figures, comic book characters, television and movie themed outfits against the old standbys of hobo, princess, or cowboy.

Costumed marches around local schools became popular, with parents, neighbors and friends coming to see the show as school children, straining at the leash to get home to really prepare for Halloween, went on parade.

Sources:

Wallace, Edyth Thomas. "New Halloween Practice Stresses Pleasure in Giving." The Oklahoman (Oct. 30, 1960): 42.

German, Hugh. "Prank suspected in State Tragedy." The Oklahoman (Nov. 13, 1960):162.

"Quiz Slated in Halloween Fatal Beating." The Oklahoman (April 13, 1961):30.

"3,200 Spooks to get Badges for Halloween." The Oklahoman (Oct. 28, 1961): 13.

Wallace, Edyth Thomas. "Safety First on Halloween is Important." The Oklahoman (Oct. 30, 1966):64.

"Goblins Ready for Halloween". The Oklahoman (Oct. 26, 1969):146.

"Halloween Tricks Turn Out Vicious." The Oklahoman (Nov. 1, 1969):7.

"Razor-in-Apple Tale False: Trick Boomerangs." The Oklahoman (Nov. 6, 1969):29.

9 The Goblins Will Get You
(1970-1979)

Mid-decade many audiences clustered around the television to see comedy sketches and the ABC television debut of the spandex and face paint rock group KISS on the "Paul Lynd Halloween Special" (1976). This should have been a clear signal that the holiday was a changing and not necessarily for the better as the holiday moved center stage into profit columns.

Deep seated suspicions and fears regarding the holiday continued as the urban legends of horrific deaths by candy were repeated each season.

These "Contamination tales", according to Nicholas Rogers, arose in the 1960's but peaked in the 1970's.

There is a little evidence, however, that any true random Halloween candy tampering has **ever** occurred resulting in the death of a child. This, despite decades of urban legends stating that very "fact." There have been no Halloween multiple deaths by drug, poison, or sharp object. News articles cried not warning each year, but no hard information was ever included to verify the dire details they listed.

Real life tragedies, however, do exist from that time.

A Pasadena, Texas boy died after eating cyanide laced candy gathered on Halloween. The poison, however, came from his own father after the man had acquired a large insurance policy on his son. Originally sentenced to die on Halloween, the Supreme Court granted a stay. The original "Candyman" finally went to his death, one of the first by lethal injection, in March 1982.

Other stories turned out to be either clear hoaxes spread by children or attempts to cover family drug use. The 'razor blade in the apple' appears to be nothing but a fraud.

A review of "Halloween Poisonings" at Snopes.com can be compared to an academic article by Bajwa, "Needle Ingestion via Halloween Carmel Apples" in the *Mayo Clinic Proceedings* (Oct. 2003). It seriously begs the question which came first: The story of the contamination or the contaminations? Did the early urban legends become self-fulfilling prophecy by century's end?

The classic horror films were castrated as they moved to television and transformed into such offerings as the inane "Munsters". In time, regular "Halloween" themed episodes of popular weekly programs and specials would, like a modern day Frankenstein's monster, take on a life of their own.

The general social and political upheaval of the 1960's was reflected in the changes in how Halloween was celebrated in the 1970's. In just as strong a manner as the revolutionary minded of the "hippies" years assaulted the traditions, values, and religions of main stream America, the 1970's saw just a forceful a movement as those elements attempted to reassert themselves.

This was also the decade of the Bicentennial and a return, or a rediscovery of traditional costumes, customs, and manners.

Values criticized and derided by the communes, free love, and other social constructions of the counter-culture, now gave rise to mainstream entertainments such as *All in the Family* and *MASH*. Affirmations of traditional values of home, friends, and family were seen in popular series such as *The Little House on the Prairie* (1976), *The Brady Bunch* (1969-), *Happy Days* (1974), *Good Times* (1974) *The Waltons* (1972) and *Laverne and Shirley* (1976).

This was also a time when the established religions, especially evangelical Christianity responded to the more worrying aspects of the new "liberality" of society. The loss of social control in general meant a loss of influence by the components of society: education, local government and religion. Suddenly, the familiar rules of social control were, like the buggy at the turn of the century, being torn apart and reassembled on the slippery slope of a steep barn. Many were at a loss as to how to cope with these social changes happening all around them.

Attempts to assert local values, curb behavior, and re-establish the 'traditional' activities did occur, however, and more community and home based events were planned.

Seen as a contributing factor in the overall devolution of society, Halloween for many heralded a submission to paganism and an invitation to rampant demonic activity within a community.

As a result, "Fall Festivals", "Reformation Day Fetes" and "Autumn Activities" were substitutes for local families and children. Civic centers, church halls, and school gyms celebrated the changing season without any of the traditional "Halloween" décor of ghosts, bats, spider webs, or simmering cauldrons. Door-to-door visits were replaced by strolls down mall storefronts and past officially sanctioned parking lots where car trunks held goodies and games

Sources

"Halloween Approaching." The Oklahoma (Oct. 22, 1971): 34.

"Treat Kills Texas Boy: Cyanide Found in Candy." The Oklahoman (Nov. 2, 1974):1.

"Halt Halloween (Letter to the Editor)". The Oklahoman ((Nov. 10, 1974):26.

Winter, Christine. "Halloween Childish Fun or Terror?" The Oklahoman (Oct. 26, 1975):102.

"Cancellation of Halloween Uncalled For." The Oklahoman (Oct. 31 1977): 17

"Ghost Hunt Good Sport: Take a Haunting Tour." The Oklahoman (May 28, 1978):102..

10 WHAT WILL YOU BE FOR HALLOWEEN?

(1980-1989)

As American culture moved into the last twenty years of the century, there was a movement to reclaim Halloween….by the adults.

The horror genre blended with the role playing, gothic chic, and counter-culture mindset of a large segment of the young adults beginning with the 1980's.

Traditional evangelical religion combated the annual spiral into what they believed to be 'witchcraft', 'paganism', and 'Satanism' with Fall Festivals and family carnivals. Yet, the move was on to make of Halloween a major economic and social anchor of the late 20th century.

Yet, the culture was shifting as post-modernism and generational shifts in society were changing forever the profile of American society.

Some extreme religious groups held a special form of the familiar 'haunted house'. These places called "Hell Houses" were designed to scare straight the wild and sinning youth. In highly dramatic, and some would say manipulative, programs they would present the dire consequences of a youth who died doing drugs, having an abortion, or doing something else perceived as wrong by that particular group (dancing, wearing inappropriate clothes, etc.).

"Demons" (costumed actors) would burst into action to swoop people out of the audience and drag them screaming and pleading to Hell.

It might be arguable as to which of the celebrations of the holiday was more frightening, the trick or treating and its attendant motifs or the sight of people being dragged, kicking and screaming, off to hell.

Nature, we are told by science, abhors a vacuum. As the streets were cleared of children scurrying about for free treats, the adults moved into claim the territory with massive parties, parades, and role playing attractions. The old haunted house now grew to include haunted fields, orchards, warehouses, and anything else large enough to lend itself to the effort.

Eclipsing selections in some years were the adult sized costumes featuring Gothic creations, vampires, mummies, and a horde of other genre favorites. Some, however, preferred to come as they were or felt they had been in a previous life.

Joining the Gothic sub-culture were neo-pagans, Wicca's, vampire wanna-be's, steam punk, and others who favored black, leather, tattoos and a plethora of piercings.

Just as the earliest communities had kept youth too long captive to their childhood without offering them meaningful avenues to exercise low-key revolt, the maturing young adults of these decades seemed to be seeking the same opportunities to spin the world around.

It could be argued that these maturing young adults were in revolt against a social construct that continued to disallow the Saturnalia festivities. Those events that allowed youth to safely try out other realities, continue to use their imaginations, role play other perspectives, and let off the steam of being controlled by the society or the community.

Halloween, as it has been defined in America, is about 'play', imagination, and wonder. It is a time to be scared and verify we are all right. It is a time to see magic and know to not have all the answers is normal .

It is a time to run, scream, and break out of the bonds of conformity in safe and accepted manners – even if it is for just one night. It is a night best suited to casual tests of courage, random acts of idiocy, light hearted fun and a keen awareness that the light of dawn will reveal all.

Costumed play among adults is at a high level and the reason is simple, it is play which keeps people inspired and motivated. It is play that keeps people young. It is play that allows people to keep from taking themselves too seriously. What can be more playful than to be someone else, sometime else and somewhere else, even if just for a night.

We need Halloween, regardless of our age, to remind us that we are all children at heart.

HALLOWEEN

The moon is high in an ebony sky.

It is spooky out here,

I cannot lie.

One foot in front of the other I go;

Stopping by the houses of people I know.

Something swoops silently over my head!

Screaming and crying:

I know I am dead!

Screech owls, horned toads, and flying bats;

With this mask, I can't see where I'm at!

Stumbling and bumbling I fall-

Bats! Now, I will have no candy at all!

Back on my feet, had anybody seen?

I had better hurry,

After all, It is Halloween!

Marilyn A. Hudson

URBAN LEGEND LINGERS ON

Around the season, it is time for tales to delight and terrify people of all ages. Popular ones are fabricated stories created around a local landmark, story, or event.

Conduct a search and you are sure to find entries like this: " The real "Cry Baby Bridge" is in.... (Kiefer, Schulter, Catoosa, Oklahoma City, and there are 3 more "fake " ones in Kellyville, etc.) The road has been completely re-routed, and the bridge is no longer standing.

The original legend goes like this: Legends states that if you go there you can sometimes hear, or see, the woman looking for her baby in the form of a glowing soft blue light. "-- See Shadowlands, or numerous other sites that lifted their information in total.

Despite some postings like this on various websites, this is one story that has to be re-evaluated with facts. Debate on the web as to the location of the "real" Crybaby Bridge in Oklahoma totally ignores the folkloric root of this tale. It is in folklore that the meaning and identification of the bridge must be found.

The story of the Crybaby Bridge always begs the question, which one? Such bridges have been identified through local legend in almost every state from New York to Ohio to Oklahoma and a few further west. Since the story did not originate in Oklahoma all claims that the "real" bridge is in

Oklahoma are simply untrue.

Experts have seen that in the western versions, there is an apparent relationship to the Hispanic tale of La Llorona. This old legend tells of a woman who drowned her children to be with her young lover, who in turn deserted her. The contemporary case of Susan Smith comes to mind as a modern example of just the same type of tragedy. This source tale may date back to pre-colonial Mexico and may even refer to an early native deity.

In these crybaby bridge tales a frequent motif is the (a)shamed daughter rejected by her father, (b) baby and woman died (either through cold or through drowning), and listeners are encouraged to remember the tale as (c) a memorial to lost innocence.

An old Irish folk song may have helped shape the development of this legend. in modern times. "Mary of the Wild Moors" is a haunting tune that has the elements of the shamed daughter, the infant baby, the rejecting father, and the lingering cry heard in the place of their death on the cold stoop of the cottage. It is moody and haunting making it a memorable tale.

Although, many areas have their haunted hollows, stretches of eerie road or spooky woods (one such place was recorded near El Reno in the early 1900's, the sight of an alleged murder). Many of these bridge tales, by comparison, seemed to have all arisen during the 1920's and 1930's.

If, as many believe, urban legends, are as much morality tales cautioning about behavior, then the often dangerous bridges of the early years, coupled with the moral threat posed by a newly independently mobile youth, could easily have led to the development of this tale and explain its enduring appeal.

Oklahoma, like Ohio, has several bridges identified as a Cry Baby

Bridge. Most have been closed down over the years, lost as roads were rerouted, or simply replaced by newer bridges. I visited one alleged sight in southwest Oklahoma County. It was down an old dirt road and had been closed for decades to motor vehicles. The metal had rusted and the wooden planks were beginning to weaken.

It crossed a narrow ravine where a tiny trickle of dirty water flowed decorated here and there with the debris of cast off appliances and car parts. An old concrete pipe in one side of the   ravine served to spill out rain water from somewhere.

In the clear light of day I could hear the wind sighing through the pipe, and knew that in the dead of night it might sound like the whimpering cries of a child, or the mournful pleas of a woman in pain.

Looking around at the lonely road, its tall stand of scrub grasses and volunteer trees, circadian hums playing background music to my musings, I wished I too had come in the night. This was something to be savored slowly and remembered before it too disappeared into myth.

One day the bridge would be gone, replaced by a staid modern bridge, and it would lose something along the way. The modern replacement bridges, with their multiple lanes of harsh glaring concrete with stable, unimaginative barriers spanning waterways the drivers can no longer even see, are no match. They are traversed by hurried traffic with no time to pause and enjoy the 'what if' or the 'just maybe's' that make life fun. Every new bridge seems designed to defy any legend, no matter how romantic and enduring, to linger.

THERE ARE PLACES PEOPLE DARE NOT GO

(An Ode to Haunted Places)

There are places people dare not go.

We sense it with shivers and wariness,

As we pass that door,

Or walk that street,

Or, find our self in that one most peculiar place.

There are places people dare not go.

They rest beneath a blanket of sorrow,

Yet their restive

Rumpled form shows,

That it is not a peaceful or a lasting sleep.

There are places people dare not go.

The gathering places of now and then,

The dark nexus of

There and here,

Where light walks and shadow speaks.

There are places people dare not go.

Hillsides suffused in pagan light,

Feral eyes shimmering bright,

Watching and waiting,

Ringing the silvered realm,

the ancient guardians.

There are places; there are places,

There are places people dare not go.

There are places we avoid, lonely places that seem to wrap melancholy arms around us.

Lonely, often desolate places, echoing with whispers of a long ago that lingers on despite time and distance. Shadowed places revealing themselves, reluctantly, only by the light of the dark.

We avoid these places. We hitch collars around our ears, duck our heads and quicken our steps as we pass. Without conscience thought, we hold our breath until that place is far behind us. We instinctively cross ourselves, or grip tighter the rabbit foot, until the face of the focus of our fear has passed from our view.

These are the places we try our best to avoid. In a small town with curving streets that speak of another time, a more gracious time, there is just such a place. Some people tell you that houses are born bad and there are some people will tell you they are like people. They learn to be bad because they absorb the habits and hungers of their inhabitants as parched ground drinks in a sweet summer rain.

No one could ever say what it was about the house on the corner that always caught people's attention. Something magnet of the extraordinary would always draw the eye or the mind. Through the years, its fading, somber Victorian tones had taken on funereal hues. A melancholy mood settled on it like a tattered shawl.

While other houses on the streets were adorned with leafy trees and flowered shrubs, the growth around this particular house seemed to sicken and lift fragile bony fingers to the skies no matter what the season. Pale and hazy, as if afflicted with cataracts, its mullioned windows seemed to be hiding dark secrets of unfathomable evil. Through the many years, its huge double doors saw a flood of families who moved in with high hopes and quickly left.

People whispered over morning cups of coffee about shrill cries heard in the night. Half-remembered tales from decades before shared in whispered tones over campfires far away from the ears of the children.

While other tales spread with a decided "tongue-in-cheek" tone of voice, mention that house, the atmosphere changed. Then the voices dropped to mere whispers and the tone turned hesitant. Most of those who knew the stories seemed eager to forget.

Try as they might to forget the ales rise from the dead of days gone by, go prowling the imaginations of each new generation, and lure them back to the shadows.   You see, try as they might the one lesson parents can never really teach is that there are places people should not go.

SOME OF THOSE WHO KEEP THE

'SPIRIT' OF HALLOWEEN ALIVE

Count Gregore aka John Ferguson. Since the 1950's to the present day the John Ferguson has entertained Oklahomans as a television personality, a movie host, and an always popular event highlight. He found his niche when he developed the "Count" and hosted a late night program featuring B movies and fine horror schlock. Loved by generations of viewers he is an always popular figure and his show was graced by many notables over the years. His story has been recorded by author Tom Fowler in <u>Count Gregore, Oklahoma Legend.</u> (2012).

Dr. Fear aka Brian Young. For a decade, starting in 2002 on station KXOK the citizens of northwest Oklahoma have been invited to the dark and mysterious laboratory of Dr. Fear as he hosts a time of appropriately inspiring radio and television program featuring rock music and original story videos. Dr. Fear, his lab assistants and various guests have been busy every week seeing what harvest of horror they can generate. Brian Young is also an up and coming horror novelist and game creator. His first novel is a unique vampire tale set in early Oklahoma. It is book one in the Silent War series, <u>De Civitate Sanguino: The City of the Bloodthirsty.</u>

Tulsa Spirit Tours, the brainchild of the Paranormal Investigators of Tulsa and Terri French White. For several years their tours of haunted Tulsa have been sold out in advance of any advertising. So popular a companion book, <u>Tulsa's Haunted History</u> was written by Terri White in 2011.

Three Rivers Museum Haunted Tours, Muskogee, Oklahoma has brought the concept of merging the past and the paranormal for a good cause. The tours are very popular and provide appreciation for the past and a thrill to go with it!

Tonya Hacker and **Tammy Wilson,** long known as *The Ghost Divas*, diversified their talents into founding two paranormal groups, hosting paranormal conferences, and teaming up to write a book, Ghostlahoma. This book is the first to focus on the ghost tales of Oklahoma.

The Ghost Teller aka Marilyn A. Hudson. The only storyteller to specialize in haunted tales, legends, and original shivery stories. Whether telling in the Overholser Mansion, the Shawnee Mall, around a blazing camp fire, in a library event room, or other venue she has thrilled listeners with her dramatic telling of tales full of history and chills.

ABOUT THE AUTHOR

Marilyn A. Hudson holds degrees in history and Information that serve her well in plumbing the deep forgotten recesses of the past to design tales rich with detail.

She is the author of *When Death Rode the Rails, Tales of Hell's Half Acre, The Bones of Summer* and co-author of the horror novel, *The Mound.*

As 'The Ghost Teller" she has toured the region sharing stories to stir the imagination and bring a chill to even the warmest day.

Contact her:
Marilyn A. Hudson marilynahudson@yahoo.com

WHORL BOOKS
www.whorlbooks.blogspot.com
whorlbooks@gmail.com

HALLOWEEN

Marilyn A. Hudson